11 SIMPLE STEPS
TO BEING A
PODCAST SENSATION

How to create, launch and run a professional podcast
from your laptop

ANGE DOVE

Author: Ange Dove
Title: 11 Simple Steps to Being a Podcast Sensation

Publisher: Proof Perfect Pte Ltd
81A Clemenceau Ave, #05-18, Singapore 239917

ISBN: 9781452851716
Independently published

TABLE OF CONTENTS

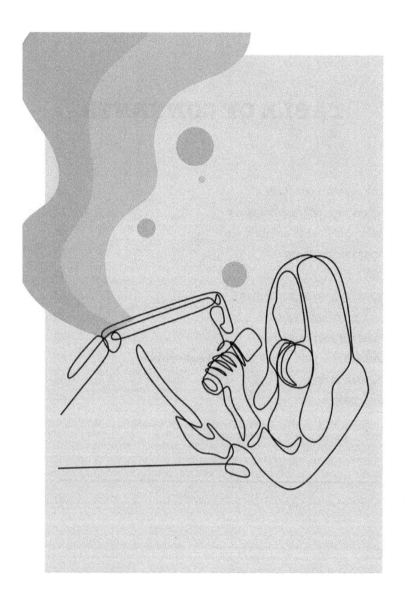

CHAPTER 1

WHY CREATE
A PODCAST?

Podcasts are a lot more popular than you may think. Perhaps you've heard the word bandied around but have never sought any out to listen to yourself. Maybe you don't even know where to find them if you wanted to listen to them. Perhaps you are the type that only consumes information via video or your social media channels like Facebook and Instagram and the thought of listening alone with no visuals is too taxing or boring. Incomprehensible even! Isn't the day of radio long gone?

Or maybe, in fact, you are an avid listener of various podcasts. You have a favourite podcast channel where you explore the delights of what is on offer in the categories you are interested in and you carve out time during your day to get your daily fix. That could be in the car on your drive to work, in the gym on the treadmill, as a background soundtrack as you do the housework, take your daily walk around the neighbourhood or work from home – maybe even as you do your homework. You are constantly listening to information to feed your mind.

Whatever way you consume or don't consume podcasts, you've begun to realise that starting your own could further your brand and your business objectives. Now is the time to do your own podcast. It's something you've been wanting to do but you aren't quite sure how to go about it.

Whatever your experience with podcasts in the past, you are here now most probably because you have a business or are thinking of starting one and you want to build your personal brand and influence across as many channels as you can. Somewhere along the way, you've found out, or someone has told you, or perhaps you've always known, that you should have a podcast.

If you are not quite convinced yet because you're wondering what the purpose of a podcast is and you're wondering why anyone would listen to them anyway, especially these days, then I urge you to read on. This could be the start of something you are going to get a kick out of for a long time to come. And the good news is that it's easier to set up than you think.

This book is here to clear up any doubts or misconceptions you may have about podcasting. It's here to tell you that podcasts are immensely popular and that they are an effective way for you to spread your influence and build your brand and authority as an expert in your niche. You see, having a podcast is a way for you to really help a special group of people – those who are waiting to hear from you and now finally can, purely because you're doing something that's audio that they can fit into their everyday busy lives. Not everyone has time for video.

To understand just how popular podcasts are, look at the statistics below taken from research by Edison Research (bit.ly/edison-infinite-dial), Nielsen (bit.ly/nielsen-podcasting), IAB (bit.ly/iab-podcasting), PwC (bit.ly/pwc-podcasting) and Pacific Content (bit.ly/pacific-content) and collated by Music Oomph! (https://musicoomph.com/podcast-statistics/).

- o As of 2020, there are more than 850,000 active podcasts and more than 30 million podcast episodes.
- o 61.2% of podcast listeners spend more time every week listening to podcasts than they do watching TV.
- o Podcast listeners spend an average of 6 hours and 37 minutes listening to podcasts every week.
- o 67% of the total podcasting audience is between 18 and 44 years old.
- o Podcasting as a whole has been growing rapidly and, as a media format, it now spans over 100 different languages across the world.

So, you can see that not only are podcasts not to be dismissed, but they can be a powerful tool in branding you and your business. If podcasting weren't effective, these podcasters would not be wasting their time doing it. Do your own research now and visit Apple and see the types of podcasts being made and who is making them. You will find a wide variety of podcast genres produced by some pretty famous names as well as many you've probably never heard of, but they command their own following.

If all of them are spending time to record a podcast on a tri-weekly, bi-weekly, or weekly basis or even if they are just doing it once a month, there's a reason that they feel it's worthwhile.

So, what are the reasons why you should be putting out a podcast, especially if you are running a business or you need to develop your personal brand because you are a coach or author? A podcast will give you "visibility" and, with it, authority in your field.

Build a brand

One of the benefits of having a podcast is that you become better branded. You become the authority in your niche. A podcast will do for your business what a book does for an author. You know how it is when an author publishes a book and it automatically gives them authority status on the topic? It lends a degree of trust. People automatically trust them because they have authored a book and they end up getting more speaking gigs, getting better exposure and being thought of as the only person to go to for the solution that they are offering in the book. It can be the same way for you with a podcast. You can build a following with a podcast purely by just showing up every week and putting valuable educational content out there around a subject matter you know about. So that's one reason why it's worth your while publishing a podcast.

Promote your offers

Another reason to publish a podcast is that you can actually use it as a great vehicle to promote your own products. So, whether you are presenting alone and giving value around the topic of your niche, or whether you bring guests on to interview, you can find opportunities within each podcast episode to promote a particular product or service of yours that you are looking to feature. It's an additional way to drive traffic or potential buyers to your offer. Someone listens to your podcast and clicks on the link to your offer and you might end up with an extra sale per click as a result of that, especially as these people will have already been warmed up to you because they've taken the time to listen to your podcast. Perhaps they listen every week and trust you as an authority. As a result, it would be much easier to convert them into paying customers than it would be for cold traffic, or people that have never heard of you before.

Expand your audience

Another reason to create a podcast is to expand your reach by expanding your audience. One great strategy to do this is by building guest interviews into your episodes. You don't have to do an interview every episode but do be aware that by having a guest speaker on, you automatically increase your audience because you are adding on their audience to your existing one.

It is worth seeking out people to interview that you share the same audience demographic with. For example, for my podcast, which serves small business owners looking to grow their business, it may be beneficial for me to interview an expert in Public Relations (PR) as this is a complementary service to mine so we will share the same type of audience. People needing their services are likely to need mine too. Make a list of people you can interview that will help bring value to your listeners and bring you additional listeners that could benefit from your services too. You will find it to be a win-win situation as your audience will benefit from additional useful information that you wouldn't normally be able to share and both of you will benefit from additional listeners you wouldn't have reached before.

There are platforms around that link podcast owners to each other much in the way Uber links passengers to drivers. I use the platform *audry.io*. On this platform, you can list your podcast for others to seek you out and you can go through the directory of other listed podcasts and directly contact each podcast owner to explore interview swaps and other opportunities.

If you are just starting out, you may want to start with those with a similar audience size to yours and work your way up as your audience expands. The owners you contact may look at your audience size first and decide the audience reach isn't worth their time. On the other hand, if you are a good fit for their audience and you have the experience that they are seeking to add value for their audience, they may be willing to have you on their podcast. Having a good One Sheet helps to get this message across. I will explain the importance of a One Sheet and how to create one in a later chapter.

Earn passive income

Another reason to have a podcast is that it can actually bring you passive income if you do it right. What do I mean by passive income? You can attract advertisers to your podcast and earn an income from the money they are willing to pay to advertise on your show. There are two ways that you can do this:

1) You can take it on completely by yourself and look for sponsors and actively seek out sponsors within your community. This means that you will be the one seeking them out, making a proposal to them and convincing them that it is worth their while sponsoring your show for the publicity it can bring them. Offer them a space on your podcast to advertise their product or service in exchange for a fee. They will also get space in your show notes as well with a link to their products or services. Your show notes are the written description of your episode that gets published with your episode.

2) If you don't have the bandwidth to go looking for sponsors, you may find that your podcast hosting platform will offer a way for you to attract advertisers automatically and you share the revenue with the platform since it does the work to bring the advertiser to you.

Obviously, for both of these advertising methods, you will need to have an attractive number of listeners tuning into your episodes.

If you are just starting out with your podcast and want to earn advertising revenue straight away, you will need to show that you already have a large audience on other platforms ready to move over and listen to your content on your podcast channel as well. But don't worry, once your podcast gets more established over time, and you authorise your podcast host to do so, you should start to attract advertisers and earn a passive income with no effort on your part.

YOUR ACTION CHALLENGE

Tick your reasons for doing a podcast and make some notes below.

- o Build your brand
- o Promote your offers
- o Expand your audience
- o Earn passive income

Make notes on each topic related to how you feel about it and what actions you are now going to take to achieve it.

Build your brand

_____
_____
_____
_____
_____
_____
_____
_____

Promote your offers

_____
_____
_____
_____
_____
_____
_____
_____

Expand your audience

_____

_____

_____

_____

_____

_____

_____

Earn passive income

_____

_____

_____

_____

_____

_____

_____

CHAPTER 2

DEFINE YOUR
PODCAST LISTENERS

In this chapter, we are going to get clear on exactly who your podcast listeners will be. Who will you be talking to? Just as with any form of communication, you need to be clear on who you are communicating with so that your topics will be of value to them. So, before you start your podcast, one of the first parts in the planning is to get very clear on who it is that you want to attract into your podcast world.

If you already have an existing business and you are already bringing in traffic into your business, the chances are that you are already very clear on who your target audience is, and you are already speaking to them through various different mediums. Your new podcast will simply be an extension of what you are already doing. That's fine and you may want to skip this chapter if that's the case. However, I'd encourage you to read through anyway because you may pick up some additional tips that will allow you to home in on your audience even further.

If you are setting up a new business and this is the first time that you are communicating to your potential audience about what it is that you know in the form of a podcast, then it is very important, before you start planning your podcast, that you identify who it is you want to have listening to you. Obviously, you need to be putting out content that will appeal to them, so you need to understand who they are and what they want to listen to. You will also need to know where to find them so that you can promote your podcast to them.

Define your listener
So, let's work on defining your ideal listener. To do this, we are going to create what we call an Avatar. This is a clear and detailed picture of your ideal customer – the one person that you can help with your products and services. Yes, one person. To create your Avatar, you need to build up a picture of one person based on a client you enjoy serving, if you have a business already, or a client that you would like to serve. In every podcast you do, you will be talking to this one person.

Create a document that defines your audience in the Action Challenge exercise at the end of this chapter. In this Action Challenge, you will see that you need to go in depth into the demographics of your listener: their personal profile, where they hang out online and what their interests and hobbies are besides the topics you cover.

There are two reasons for this:

1) You need to understand their interests and motivations so that you can create content that will be valuable to them and help them in some way.
2) Once you understand their interests and research around what other types of content that they enjoy consuming, you will be able to target them through ads and bring them over to explore your show.

Add value through your content

What is the value that you will be able to deliver in exchange for them giving you their precious time in listening to your podcasts? This is an important point to consider, and you can only answer this when you know who you are catering to.

o   Are you a proven expert in your field?
o   Are you someone who's done what they want to do?
o   Do you have a proven track record?
o   Are you the person able to help them in your particular niche?
o   What problem will you solve for them?

You need to gain their trust so that they will tune in to your show. You need to think about what value you will be giving an exchange for the time they will be investing in you. This has to be crystal clear in your communications around your podcast.

o   What is it about?
o   What are they going to learn from you?
o   How is it going to help them in their life or their business?

Speak their lingo

Consider also how you will speak about these problems. To bring your ideal listener in, you need to be speaking their language. What I mean by this is that you need to describe their problems in the same way they do. It is likely that they will not use the industry terms or jargon that you do. For example, in marketing, your customers may not talk about "traffic" but use the words "potential customers" instead. So, you need to use those words too. I recommend that you do some research around who they are, where they hang out and what other things they're listening to or they're watching so that you can speak in the same language.

Social listen

If you have existing customers, ask them what they want to learn. Do a survey and take note of the phrases they use in their reply and incorporate them into your communications. If you don't yet have customers, join groups on social media where they are hanging out and ask them questions to find out what it is that they are wanting to learn. Visit forums and groups and take note of the way they communicate and specifically the questions they want answered.

What's missing from the information that they are currently consuming?

- How do they talk?
- What words do they use when they give their answers?
- What names do they give to things and how do they express their feelings?
- How do they express the things that are going on around them?

This will give you a lot of ideas, and ammunition if you like, as to how you're going to communicate in your podcast. You want to be speaking to address and answer their pain and give a solution based on the words that they use themselves.

Do this research well and you will find that it is much easier for you to connect with your audience. Yes, you want to be authentic and who you are, and you want to speak as you would normally speak. It is very important to be yourself. But at the same time, be aware of the language that they use and the issues they have so that you can create that important connection and trust. Speak to their issues and seek to solve their problems.

Centre your communication around transformation
Once you understand your target listener, identify the kind of transformation that you're going to be delivering for them. It would be ideal if you can communicate that on the title of your podcast. We will talk about titles in more depth in a later chapter. But be thinking about it now as you do your audience research.

In order to deliver transformation, you need to know where your listener is now in their transformation journey and where they want to be. Talk about that transformation in your podcasts and describe how you will get them there or how they will get there based on what they'll be listening to in your podcast.

- How will you help to drive that transformation for them?
- What kind of information are they missing now that you can give them in your podcast that will help them to make that change and get to where they want to be?

It is critical that you communicate this information correctly and clearly because that is the reason why they will actually listen to your podcast. But before you can do any of that, you need to know who it is you are talking to. Do your research. Social listen. Get to know your listener well.

Find your listeners
As I mentioned earlier, another reason you need to know your listener is that you will need to be able to

find them online to be able to market to them and make them aware of your podcast. You need to know where these listeners are hanging out.

By defining your listeners, you will have a better understanding of where to find them when it comes to marketing your podcast to them. Determine what kind of platforms they are hanging out on so that you can reach them. Are you going to advertise on Facebook or is your target demographic younger and they'll be found on Instagram? Are you speaking Business 2 Business? If so, LinkedIn may be the place to find your listeners.

Target their interests and demographic in your targeted ads and, in your ads, speak to their pain, promise a solution to their problem. You can see now how all this research on your target listeners comes together to help you find them and deliver value to them.

YOUR ACTION CHALLENGE

Understand your ideal listener.

Building an audience for your podcast becomes easier when you have the exact kind of person in mind. Let's create your Avatar now. Resist the temptation to include everyone. Think of a client you've really enjoyed serving or someone who really could use your help.

1. Are they male or female?

2. Give them an appropriate real name.

3. How old are they?

4. Are they married or single?

5. Do they have children and if so how old are they?

6. What is their job and income?

7. What are their interests and hobbies?

8. Add a photo of your Avatar. It can be a real person, or an image taken from a magazine that represents the type of person you are targeting.

9. What do they want from your services? What conversations usually come up? Survey your existing or potential clients. With this information, write down below what your unique selling proposition is for your ideal listener. Why are you the only logical choice?

_____

_____

_____

_____

_____

_____

_____

10. It's also a useful exercise to list out what you DON'T want in a client or listener – an Anti-Avatar. Who doesn't need your services? Who can you not add value to? Who would be wasting their time and yours?

_____

_____

_____

_____

_____

_____

_____

CHAPTER 3

CRAFT YOUR "GET SEEN" FORMULA

Now it's time to discuss how you craft your Get Seen formula, which means creating the brand for your podcast, the visible aspects of it and everything else you need to know about the branding of it.

So, how are you going to brand your podcast?

Name your podcast

Let's start by giving your podcast a name. It will be ideal if the name makes it crystal clear at first glance exactly what your podcast is about. You are competing with many other titles out there, so don't make the listener guess as they are browsing the library of podcasts available. You want them to click on yours.

Brainstorm a few names and see what is appropriate and what stands out the most for you. If you're a bit divided about certain titles that you could give to your podcast, you might want to put it into your existing social media platform and ask your community what they think. You could say:

Hey, I'm launching a podcast and need your opinion about its title. Which one do you think sounds better to you? Which speaks more to you?

See what comments come back. If you get an overwhelming response for one, then obviously, that's the one you should be going with. If opinion seems pretty divided and there is no clear winner, either go with your gut instinct and pick the one you know is right for you or go back to the drawing board and think and test again until you have a clear winner.

Your podcast name could be the name of your existing brand if you have one, so that makes it very easy for you to just name your podcast based on that brand. The advantage there is that your existing audience will already be familiar with it. But if you don't have that yet, you need to start creating a name that your audience will get familiar with and that will speak to them as to the podcast that will give them the information that they need to make their transformation.

Before you settle on a name, do some research on the podcasts already out there and see how names are commonly formatted. You will notice that the names are short. You don't have a lot of space on the visual tile people see when they browse podcasts. So, keep that in mind as you confirm your podcast's name. Keep it short.

Make it unique
Once you have decided on a name, do some research online to make sure the name isn't already taken. Again, go back and have a look at the podcast platforms that are out there. Do a search for the name or the keywords in the name that you are thinking of and see what comes up. Don't just rely on the names in existing podcasts. Google the name as well and see what comes up. You don't want to be competing with the same name as some brand that is already well established, especially as they might have already trademarked the

name. If the name is already taken, then obviously you need to go back to the drawing board and think again about the title to use.

You don't want to be wasting your time and your money creating a brand for your podcast and then at the end just before you launch (or worse, after you launch it) find that there is something similar being done already.

Protect your brand
When you have found your name and you have established that nobody else is using it and it looks like a great name for your podcast, you can consider protecting the brand if you are serious about your podcast and you know that you're going to be doing this for some good time into the future, and you know it is going to strengthen your brand. Consider registering the name and the brand design as a trademark. To do this, go to your local trademark government website or contact a trademark lawyer and enquire about how to protect your podcast name.

I mentioned above registering the brand design as well. Let's look now at creating the visual brand of your podcast show.

Build your podcast's visual identity
What is your brand going to look like in terms of its colours and the visuals that you are going to create around it? You want a visual identity so that people can get familiar with the way your podcast looks and you stand out from the crowd.

This requires you going back to the list of existing podcasts again to see how their tiles have been designed. What are common elements among all? Especially look at those you will be competing against.

- o What are they doing?
- o What are they saying?
- o What does their brand look like?
- o What colours are they using?
- o What kind of visuals are they using?
- o How will you stand out against them?

This is an extreme example, but just imagine that all of the podcast designs you see in your niche are all using illustrations on the design for their podcast and they are not using the speaker's face. If everyone's doing illustrations, you would stand out if you didn't do an illustration but used your own image.

Or what if the majority of tiles in your niche where quite busy, would a minimalist design on your tile get more attention?

Look too at the colours being used by others. How can your tile stand out by being a different colour?

Stand out, but appeal too
It's important to look at what other people are doing and then think of how you can do it a little bit differently so that you don't look the same as everybody else. You don't want to be creating something visually that has nothing to do with your niche or topic though. Yes, you want to stand out, but you don't want to stand out for the wrong reasons. It still needs to be something that your listener will be able to recognise as something they want to listen to. If the visual doesn't appeal to them in that way, if it just doesn't look like this podcast is going to talk about that topic, then you need to rethink the design.

Getting your podcast tile designed

Now that you've seen the other tiles out there, your competition, is designing your own tile something you think you can handle yourself, or will you outsource the task to a professional?

If you are not artistically inclined, I would recommend that you outsource the creation of the visual brand or translation of the existing brand to a professional graphic designer.

Outsourcing the design

You can outsource the work to one of the many local graphic design agencies in your area. If you are already using a graphic design company or you are using a freelancer to do graphic design in other aspects of your business, then you can obviously use the same designer. They are trusted and they know your brand, so they will be able, with not a lot of effort, to come up with a suitable tile for you based on your existing branding.

If you are starting a new business or you don't have a designer to fall back on, not to worry. There are plenty of choices online for you to go to. Let's go through a few of your options.

Fiverr

The cheapest option open to you is Fiverr. This is a site you can go to and post your job description and designers will bid to do the job for you. Based on the site's name, the fees will be very cheap, but a word of caution – you usually get what you pay for, but you can get lucky. The advantage of Fiverr is that, because the fees are low, you can employ several designers on the platform, give them all the same brief, see what they come back with and choose the best design. You will have to pay each of them of course. But because the prices are very much cheaper anyway, it's worth the investment to get a few different ideas.

Upwork

Upwork is a similar site but this is where professional designers will display their work. You can expect to pay more, but this should give you a sense of comfort. You can also see the artist's past portfolio and read testimonials from past clients. So, you are not going in blind. In the rare instance where the artist misrepresented their work in their portfolio, and you don't get what you ordered, you can claim back the deposit that Upwork is holding in escrow (see next paragraph) for you.

People Per Hour

People Per Hour works in a similar way as Upwork and it's a site that I use regularly. On both sites, you would be expected to pay a deposit to get the work going and this is held in escrow by the platform until you agree to release it when you are happy with the work done. If the work does not come up to standard, you can ask for a refund if you reject the work completely.

So, when it comes to outsourcing your design, you have the choice of outsourcing to a professional designer, either someone you have already worked with or someone on any of these online platforms. Remember, on the online platforms, you can sift through the testimonials that they have from past clients and you can look at the past work. So, it's not like you're choosing blind. You will have some information that will help you to select the right designer and, if the work doesn't come back as expected, you can ask for a refund of the money placed in escrow.

The added benefit is that, once you find a designer you like, you can use them again for future projects.

Do it yourself

The other option is you do it yourself, if you are artistically inclined and have faith in your own design skills. If so, you have probably already formulated a rough design in your mind's eye. So, it makes sense to do it yourself. If you aren't familiar with Adobe Creative Suite, or find it too complicated to learn, there is a solution that anyone can use, and that is Canva. It doesn't require any technical skills and, with the templates it provides, you'll be creating professional-looking designs in no time.

Canva

Canva is really easy to use. It's a drag-and-drop facility found at canva.com. Have a look at the quick training video on the site and you should be good to go. It has a wide choice of design templates, images, graphics and fonts you can use, and the design possibilities are endless.

Once you are ready to work on Canva, you can start to create your podcast tiles. So, how do you make a start? First of all, look at the size of the canvas you need to use. You need to make your tiles a specific size to fit into the standard podcast displays. The way to do this is to select your canvas size on Canva by selecting the custom size setting. Key in the desired size and Canva will bring up a blank canvas for you to start working on. You will need to build two sizes of tiles – a square one and a landscape rectangle one. The reason for this is that, for most of the podcast platforms, your visual will be displayed as a square tile but for those looking on some screens or larger displays, it will appear as a rectangle. So, you need to upload both types into your podcast hosting platform.

Square tile
Your square tile needs to 1,400 x 1400 pixels at the minimum and 3,000 x 3,000 pixels at the maximum. Any number you choose between these numbers is fine as long as it is square. The final downloaded file needs to be 72 dpi and in RGB colour space.

Rectangle tile
Your rectangle tile needs to be 16:9 aspect ratio and at least 1,400 pixels wide. So, if the width is 1,400 pixels, that will be your 16 ratio, then the height needs to be the 9 ratio equivalent or 787.50 pixels. Work on your square tile first and as long as you select the paid version of Canva, you can easily copy and resize the finished design to the rectangle size and Canva will automatically resize and shift the design for you. You may need to do some minor adjustments to get the design exactly right in the rectangle version. If you don't have the paid version of Canva, the resizing option will not be available, and you will need to recreate the design from scratch in the new size.

Create a brand toolkit
To start the design, you may have some ideas already, especially if you have an existing brand. You will need to follow the brand identity quite faithfully in that case. Ask your designer for the exact colour codes of your brand colours and you can key these directly into Canva to faithfully replicate the colours. Store your

colours in the Brand Toolkit folder you will find in your Canva account so that you can always go back and refer to them. You can do the same with your brand fonts to make sure you are always using the correct fonts. You can also store your logo in your toolkit so that you have everything you need at hand to stay true to your brand.

If you don't already have an existing visual brand identity, then you are free to build on Canva from scratch. You will start with one page or canvas, but you can always copy the design you do onto a new page to make changes and play around with the design. Create a few pages and play around until you see the design you like. Once you have settled on a look, save the fonts, colours and logo in your Canva brand toolkit for future reference.

Working in Canva

Within Canva, you can drag in photos and graphics, add text, selecting from a wide choice of font styles and add any colours and shapes you choose. If you are really stuck for ideas, browse through the many design templates Canva offers and use them as your starting point.

Once you have one design done, don't stop there. Duplicate it and make changes to see what other possibilities come up. Play around until you see a design that you really like and that really works for you and you think *yeah, that's great*. Then you have the design of the tile for your podcast!

As mentioned previously, do go to the existing podcasts that are out there to have a look at how they do their tiles. One thing to make note of is how they do their tiles in terms of the amount of words on the tile and the empty space around the visual elements. The tiles are going to show up quite small on the screen anyway, so you don't want to be putting a lot of text on your tile because it is just not going to be readable. So, make sure that you choose a fairly short title or if it's a longer title, they are the only words you will put on the tile.

Decide whether you want to put your name on it or not. Some people do and some don't. Take a look at what's out there, how it can be done, and which approach you prefer. There are different ways to do it. Your podcast could be your name, or it could be something completely different. So, it's up to you how you want to position it and how you design it as well.

Decide based on what you see, how you see yours fitting in. Have a look at colours and which colours tend to pop and which don't. Personally, I would keep it as simple as possible. You want to create a lot of blank space within it so that it doesn't look too cluttered and so that, most importantly, it's easy to read and it stands out on the screen among all the others.

Bold colours usually help quite a lot as these stand out. However, you will probably also see some tiles work well in very muted colours. So, it really depends on your brand and how you want to be seen and how you want to be seen against the competition. Take the inspiration from all the other tiles you see and then create your own.

Apple restrictions
One final word on designing your podcast tile - and this is specifically for when it goes up on the Apple platform.

- It must not make reference to Apple or any Apple products.
- It can't mention the Apple brand or any related Apple brand products

o It can't show any Apple products. So, for example, you can't have a picture of a person holding an iPhone.

If you violate this rule, your podcast will not be accepted to the Apple platform. So, make sure that you're not promoting any Apple products visually on the tile for your podcast at all.

Promotional materials

Now that you have your podcast tile designed, let's turn our attention to the other visuals you will need to promote your podcast. One extra thing you will need to build is a landing page to promote your podcast.

Your landing page should explain:
o what the podcast is
o why a podcast
o who will benefit from listening to it
o what the benefits are they will get from it
o why it is they need to listen to this podcast
o what it's going to do for them in terms of their transformation

That's all the points we covered in the first chapter about why have a podcast in the first place, and why yours is going to help them. It is important to communicate this key message in your landing page. Communicate the obvious benefits of learning from you via podcast rather than video. They are able to listen on the go, on the move. They don't have to stop and watch a video. They can just consume your content while they're going about their busy day, whether they're driving in the car, they're doing the ironing, doing the housework, they're running on a treadmill in the gym, etc. They can listen to your podcast and get some education at the same time.

Building your landing page

How do you design your landing page? Be sure to use the same kind of fonts, colours and graphics and the key messaging that you put on your tile. Keep the designs consistent. Be sure to include your list opt-in form in your landing page. This way you can send them a welcome email, and this will include the link to the podcast for them to go and subscribe.

What tools do you need to create a landing page and your list?

Your landing page tool will depend very much on your experience in building landing pages. If you have a WordPress site and your theme includes a landing page template, you could create new pages there. Otherwise you are going to need a landing page builder. Look up the phrase *landing page builder* in your browser and explore the suggestions that come up. I used to find Instapage very useful. It is an easy drag and drop platform and it's easy to have a landing page up in a few minutes. Another popular option is ClickFunnels.

You may find that the app you choose as your list builder, such as Mailchimp or Active Campaign, has a landing page function built in so you can combine two in one. All of the apps mentioned except WordPress are provided on a subscription-based model, meaning you will need to pay a set fee each month to keep using them. Mailchimp is free up to a certain number of subscribers to your list.

I've used all the above at various points in the past, then I found a few platforms that simplified all of my marketing into one easy tool – Simplero is one, and a newly launched platform GrooveFunnels is another. I can very quickly build landing pages to opt people into a list and then send them automated email campaigns based on their interest in what they signed up for. It also allows me to create a thank you page. I usually use this to invite them to my Facebook Group Community as well. Think of multiple ways you can cross promote your own social media platforms including your podcast.

Promote every chance you get

Once you set up your podcast, you should be promoting it everywhere. Places you can place a link include:

- o your email signature,
- o thank-you pages, and
- o all of your social media platforms and groups.

Another way I promote my podcast and quite a few other avenues into my world is through an app called Linktree. I place a single link on my email signature to my Linktree page and this provides multiple links to various places I want to send people, including my podcast. But I also send them to Amazon to buy my books and to my groups to take part in challenges, etc. Linktree is free if you don't want to add your visual branding to the page.

Your podcast introduction

Now that you are ready with your visual assets, it's time to work out how you are going to introduce your podcast to the world – what you are going to put on your landing page, etc.

You need a boilerplate intro that you will use as the spoken intro to each episode in your podcast intro section, and as the introduction in your show notes. People need to know what your podcast is and who it is for. What are they going to hear?

This introduction needs to be a very concise introduction to what your podcast is about. Follow this formula:

(Name of your podcast) is for (target listener) who want to (transformation you will deliver for them).

Here is an example of my podcast intro.

Welcome to the Build a Purposeful Profitable Business Doing What Your Absolutely Love podcast, hosted weekly by Ange Dove, Your Business Fairy Godmother, professional copywriter, published author and business owner of 20 years. In every episode, Ange will deliver useful bitesize insights to help you find your voice, position your value, demystify the marketing tech and run your business on your terms.

Your One Sheet
Now that you are clear on the purpose of your podcast, your target listener and your brand identity, you can now create your One Sheet.

Your One Sheet is, as the name suggests, a single sheet that promotes your podcast to potential advertisers and podcast owners you are seeking to swap interview slots with.

Your One Sheet should include:
- o   your brand visual identity and logo
- o   a clear picture of you that communicates your brand
- o   a hook that clearly communicates what your podcast does for its target listener
- o   a short bio of you, about a third of the page
- o   interview topics you are willing to cover

- o sample questions your interviewer can ask
- o your contact details
- o links to relevant social media sites and websites you own

Here is my One Sheet as an example

YOUR BUSINESS FAIRY GODMOTHER

What if you could build a purposeful, profitable business doing what you absolutely love, simply by sharing what you know?

Ange Dove is the founder and CEO of content marketing agency Proof Perfect in Singapore and learning portal MarketSMART Learning Hub, as well as a professional copywriter, mentor, coach, author and mother to two amazing young adults.

Over nearly 20 years of running her company, the first and longest-standing copywriting agency in Singapore, Ange saw a pattern in the challenges her small business owner clients faced. Based on her conversations with them, she formulated her signature Get Ready Get Seen Get Business system to help business owners, coaches and authors, even the non-tech-savvy, brand themselves, package their value, create their products based on their genius, and market their offers to their tribe of willing buyers. She facilitates transformation for her clients by simplifying the complex and knowing that everything is workoutable if you are willing to do the work.

To further support her clients wanting to leave the 9-to-5 and find their value and freedom running their own business, just as she had, Ange also hosts her How to Build and Run a Purposeful Profitable Business Doing What You Absolutely Love podcast.

INTERVIEW TOPICS

Find Your Voice - You are good enough and there is an audience for you
Build Your Brand - How to create an authentic, unique brand just being you
Systemise Your Business - How to prepare for growth and a team even as a solopreneur
Business in the New Normal - How to operate your business location-free on the cloud, and build a global team with virtually no fixed overheads
My 5G Approach to Copywriting™ - How to get paid while you sleep

SAMPLE QUESTIONS

How can you monetise what you know?
Why does being authentic trump being slick every time?
How do you create consistency in your branding and why is it important?
How does systemising your business prepare your business for growth?
What are the things that can be systemised in any business?
Why is your brand important when it comes to building a team?
What are the five elements of good copywriting?
What should you avoid in your writing if you want to convert browsers to buyers?

@AngeDove
@YourBusinessFairyGodmother
@Ange.Dove
@AngeDove
@Angedove
AngeDove.com
angee@angedove.com
+65 6970 9200

YOUR ACTION CHALLENGE

Write the name of your podcast.

Write the introduction to your podcast here.

_____

_____

_____

_____

_____

_____

_____

Your brand identity
List your fonts names and colour codes.

Your promotion plan
Describe what materials you will use to promote your podcast and the dates by which you will have these created.

Materials   **Date**

_____   _____

_____   _____

_____   _____

_____   _____

_____   _____

_____   _____

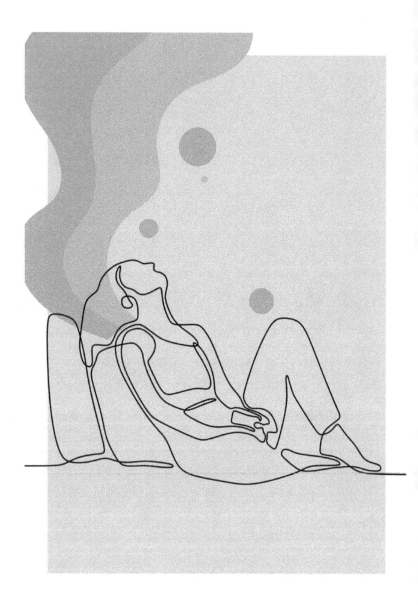

CHAPTER 4

FIND YOUR LISTENERS

Now that you have designed your podcast and have the promotional materials to promote it, you need to establish where you are going to place your promotional materials so that they get in front of your target listener.

This needs to happen even before you launch your podcast. Market to them to tease them about the show and announce that it's coming soon.

So, where do you find your listeners?

This all stems from what we said in chapter 2 about knowing who your listener is because if you know who they are, what their interests are and where they hang out, you will know where to find them so that you can advertise and promote to them.

If you have an existing audience, obviously you can advertise or promote to that audience and share the exciting news that you now have a podcast to help them.

- o Send an email to your existing audience and explain about your podcast and invite them over to subscribe.

o   Announce your podcast launch on your social media pages and groups and post regularly to garner interest up to the launch date.

These existing contacts are warm audiences. You should be able to get them over to your podcast at least. But obviously you need to grow your audience list and it needs to be not just your existing audience who know you but new people who could benefit from learning from you.

The best way to do that is through paid advertising. Facebook is a great way for you to target your exact demographic. You can set up ads that will entice people over to your podcast via your landing page and help you grow your list.

The money is in your list

You've probably heard the saying that the money is in your list. This is because most people won't act upon first contact. So, if you can save their contact details, you can communicate with them over and over with different offers until they take action. The money is actually in the follow up. You need a list to be able to follow up. So, make sure that whatever you're doing advertising wise, you are collecting contact details and adding them to your list before sending them over to your podcast. You do this through what is called an opt-in.

Building your list

Offer an opt-in

An opt-in is a great way to build your list. Offer a free download on your landing page. This should be short to consume, like a checklist, a guide of a few pages, a quiz, an insider secrets report, etc. You can then send them an email with details of your podcast and a link to go listen and subscribe.

Interview guests

Another way that you can build your list is to appear on other people's podcast and have them on yours. You benefit from having their audience listen to you too. Make sure you have some gift they can consume so you can capture their details on your list through an opt-in you can send them to.

Paid advertising

In terms of Facebook advertising, as we have covered, you can really narrow down your niche and advertise to a very select audience and this is why in the earlier chapters I stressed so much about knowing who your listener is and knowing where to find them because if you know the types of information they consume, who they consume it from, and what platforms they hang out on, you can target them and get their attention by putting forward your offer. Target your Facebook ads to those people.

YOUR ACTION CHALLENGE

How will you build your audience? List the suggestions in the chapter that you can use to grow your audience before and after you launch your podcast.

1.

2.

3.

4.

5.

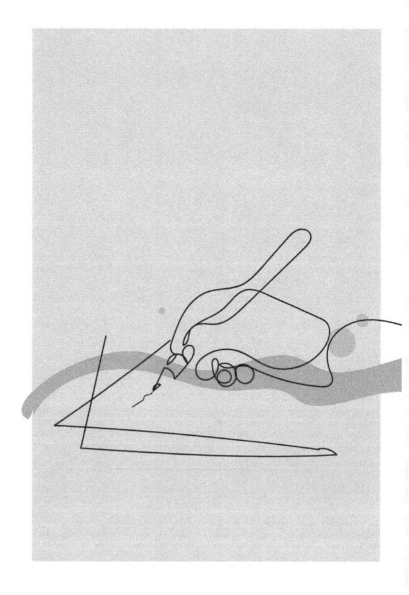

CHAPTER 5

PLAN YOUR
PODCAST CONTENT

Let's turn now to the content you will deliver in your podcast. Setting up a podcast means you need to commit to providing ongoing content on a regular basis. When you first start a podcast, that can seem pretty daunting. Common fears are: What if I run out of ideas?

Now the good thing is that once you put your mind to brainstorming the content that you could provide, you'll find that you are never going to run out of ideas. There are definitely things that you can do to plan out content that is never-ending. There are so many things that you could actually be talking about in your niche.

If you plan it right, you're going to have the nice challenge of having so much content, you'll wonder how you can ever cover it all! That's a great problem to have and we'll get you there in this chapter by having you think about what content you could put out.

Let's get started, shall we? First of all, what I want you to do is to brainstorm ideas. Do this on a piece of paper rather than on the screen. There is something about writing on paper that frees the mind and lets ideas flow through. If you relax and just let your thoughts wonder and don't restrict yourself in any way, you'll find that you can fill the page and more.

Step 1

Brainstorm all the possible topics that you deal with in your niche. What are your main areas of expertise? There's no right or wrong answer at this point just brainstorm ideas and don't censor yourself. Censoring is the worst thing you can do. This is a time when you're just freeing your mind. So, anything that comes to mind no matter how silly it might sound, just put it down on paper. Write down absolutely everything that comes to your mind. Don't edit. Don't rub anything out. Don't cross anything out. Just keep going and keep brainstorming, forming all the possible broad topics that you can think of to talk about.

As an example, for me, my broad topics are:

- o Branding
- o Positioning
- o Copywriting
- o Marketing
- o Marketing tech tools
- o Business automation

Step 2

Once you have brainstormed your list of main topics, see if you can group some ideas together or whether you need to divide some still further. Aim to have about five to six key areas of focus. These are your main buckets of content.

Step 3

OK. Now it's time to fill those buckets to the brim with content ideas.

Focus on one bucket, one main topic, at a time.

For your first bucket, go through another brainstorming session in the same way on paper and let your ideas flow. Again, don't censor yourself. Just aim to fill the page. 50 ideas should be a minimum. Once you feel you have exhausted ideas, move to the next bucket and a fresh piece of paper.

Do this for each of the buckets.

Step 4
Now look at all the ideas that you jotted down and see how you can organise them into subtopics so you can group them together and you have a sense of organisation over your content.

Step 5
Now look at each idea again and see if you can spring further ideas off them.

Each idea could be an episode of your podcast. How many episodes have you got now and how long would it take for you to release them all? A few years at least? And that's not even counting episodes where you will have guests! As you start to build your podcast and you start to record and get some feedback, you're going to think of other ideas as well.

Use this large list of ideas as a fallback for when you don't have things to podcast about. But you will find that other ideas pop up depending on what clients ask you or what is going on in your industry or in current events. So be prepared to keep things fluid. Your next podcast topic might be a spark of an idea you just had that is relevant to your audience or just might be something of interest to you that you've picked up that week. And then of course, there are your interviews, if you're going to do podcasts with interviews. Then that person's topic is going to consume that particular episode. So, can you see now that you won't run out of content at all?

Always deliver value

Of course, before you confirm content for any episode, it has to pass the Audience Value test. If you aren't sure if a piece of content will interest your audience, the best thing to do is to ask them. That can be your existing clients if you have them, or followers of your social pages or groups. Simply test out your ideas and see the response or just ask them directly what they want help with. Add what comes back to your bucket of ideas.

What you could also do is create one podcast, record it and just send it out to a few select people that you trust. Ask them for their feedback and act on what comes back.

Always bring the topics back to what your people want to know about. What information do they need so that they can transform from the Point A where they are now to Point B where they need to be. From the work you have already done, you know who your avatar is, you know where they are now, you know where they need to be and you know what steps they need to take to get to Point B. Make sure your content goes some way to moving them along in their journey, pushing them towards that transformation, little by little.

YOUR ACTION CHALLENGE

List your main topics along the top row of this table and record the content ideas you have come up with under each. You will need more paper!

CHAPTER 6

SELECT YOUR PODCAST FORMAT

There are different formats that you can choose for your podcast depending on the experience you want to create for your listener and how much time and energy you have to give to creating your podcasts each week or month.

Flying solo

You can decide that you want to go alone and do it solo. This means that you are the sole presenter and nobody else, and you are the person talking in every single episode. With this format, you won't have any guest speakers. It's just going to be you on your own sharing your teachings and being the guru and guide for your audience. Your podcast is, therefore, an extension of everything else you are doing around your existing brand, your coaching and your teaching around your niche area of expertise.

When is it good to pick this format of presenting solo? I've already hinted at it above. If you are wanting to extend the reach of your existing brand and gain a wider audience or you are wanting to give your existing audience a new option in the way they consume your information, maybe in a more on-the-go format, then a solo podcast is a great way to do that.

It's natural with this goal for you to be the sole presenter. You have a pre-existing audience and they are expecting to hear and are used to hearing from you. This is what they want and is why they are following you. Your podcast is an extra way for you to give your value to them.

Being a solo presenter of your podcast, you need to plan your content around what it is that you teach and just make sure that each episode gives your listeners something manageable for them to digest, some step-by-step information that they can consume and enjoy on the move.

Co-hosting

If you have a team, this could be an excellent format for your business brand. It also has the added benefit of taking some of the time and preparation pressure off you because the podcast is shared.

You can either take it in turns to do episodes or you can all present together in a kind of radio breakfast show chat format, where you've got DJs bantering with each other. This is quite an entertaining way to do a podcast, especially as it lends itself nicely to humour and debate. The onus doesn't fall completely on you. It's not up to you alone to entertain the audience.

When you have a co-partner or two on the show, it's easier to make the episodes more engaging because you will tend to have a natural conversation going between you. You can very quickly build a strong brand around that if the camaraderie works.

Of course, you don't have to all appear on the show together. You can divide the podcast into two or three of you doing different types of episodes each if each of you is known for a different area of expertise. Your listeners will come to know to expect what they're going to listen to, based on who the speaker is for each particular episode.

The beauty of podcasting is that it's completely up to you how you want to handle it. It's your brand and your show. There are no hard and fast rules. Do it the way that you want to do it.

Guest interviews

In this format, you will feature a guest in every episode. This gives you some added work as you will need to line up a guest for each episode, which can be added pressure, especially if you have committed to a set schedule and need to fill each slot.

If you are thinking right now that this is too risky or too much work, let's consider the obvious benefits of this format. When you have a guest on each week, you aren't just broadcasting to your existing audience. You are broadcasting to theirs as well. So effectively you get to speak to a new audience every week. It's a great way to grow your visibility, your brand and your list.

Of course, as hinted at above, this means you need to find a guest for every episode. Be sure that you have a strategy and the resources to do this before you decide on this format. As mentioned in an earlier chapter, there are platforms out there that team up podcasters for interviews. I use *audry.io* and find it very useful. I have my virtual assistant (VA) research the podcasts and present me with options. I confirm those I am interested in connecting with either for me to be a guest on their show, for them to be a guest on my show or both. My VA then contacts the podcast owner through audry.io and attaches a link to my One Sheet. For those that reply positively, I take over the conversation and we book the shows. If you have the resources to outsource the initial contacting, you should be able to have a good line-up of guests for each episode without much input of your time.

As your podcast grows in followers and reputation, you will find more people will be seeking you out and you'll be flooded with One Sheets to review.

The added benefit of course of this type of format is that you give your listeners variety with every episode. They'll tune into each episode not really knowing what to expect, which may be an added draw to them. But be careful not to get lost in the process. It's still your show and your brand, so make sure you give yourself airtime as well.

Mixed format
This format may appeal to you if you don't want to be tied to any particular format and enjoy the flexibility to do your episodes with what you have to hand that week, or you want to give your listeners the variety of the occasional guest speaker episode interspersed between your regular solo presented episodes. This lessens the pressure of having to line up a guest speaker for every episode as well. It won't seem odd if a guest presenter slot falls through at the last minute. You can do an episode with you presenting solo and your audience would be none the wiser.

Your show is so mixed that your listeners will just assume that it was part of the plan if you don't have a guest. Of course, if you promote your episodes in advance and need to reschedule a guest, the change of plan will be obvious.

Deciding on the episode length

The next thing you want to think about is what the length is going to be of every episode. You want to try to keep your episodes within a certain range of length so that your listeners can plan their day around them. If they are used to you doing 15-minute episodes and you suddenly drop an hour-long show, it's going to be hard for them to consume in the way they normally do. If you do this too often, you may lose listeners who want the stability of fixed length episodes.

So, if you decide to do quick 10-minute episodes with a short blast of information each time, then you want to keep it that way as your audience will come to expect and plan for it. It works the other way too. If you commit to doing hour-long episodes and you suddenly present a 15-minute one, this may throw out your listeners' plans. I've been told by several podcast listeners that they plan their podcast listening into their daily routine and will, for example, choose to listen to hour-long podcasts when doing their daily hour-long walk each morning. They fit their daily education in at the same time as going for their walk and are occupied for the full length of their walk. Imagine them planning to listen to your podcast as per usual and the episode suddenly coming to an end after 15 minutes. They would have nothing else planned to listen to during their walk. So, do consider your listeners and how they depend on the reliability of the length of your episodes when planning their day.

Having your episodes roughly or even exactly the same length each episode will also make your podcast look professional and well planned. The length itself can be up to you but keep it consistent. There are no hard and fast rules about the length a podcast should be. Some are 15 minutes, some half an hour, and some an hour or more. The longer the time you choose, obviously the more content you will have to find to fill that space. A

15-minute episode is a lot easier to fill than an hour episode. But you also need to consider whether 15 minutes is long enough to get your message across, especially if you have a guest speaker.

In short, the format you decide upon will also help to determine the length of each show. If you decide you are going to feature guests, then you should buffer for at least half an hour per episode if not 45 minutes. Whereas if you're a solo presenter, 10- to 15-minute episodes may be just your thing.

It may be quite natural as a solo presenter for you to start your show as a 15-minute episode show then as you grow in confidence and find your rhythm, you might end up going longer on a regular basis and, before you know it, all your episodes might be an hour long.

You may find that you become very comfortable at doing longer episodes and you don't want to do 15-minute episodes anymore because you find you're not giving your readers the value that you want to give. Or vice versa. You may find that it's quite tiring to do long episodes and you want to just cut it down to short snippets of 15 minutes per episode. There's no wrong way to go about it.

Deciding on the frequency
Next, consider how often you can commit to putting out episodes. They should be regular in the same way as they should be roughly the same length. You might decide to make it a monthly affair. Or it could be weekly, or even twice or three times a week.

So, have a think about the time that you want to put into doing your podcasts and what you can comfortably commit to. I would advise at the beginning that you don't overcommit. So, don't get really excited about doing three episodes a week and launching on that then running out of steam and finding that you can't come up with the content or that your schedule doesn't allow you to realistically do three times a week. Get into your stride first with shorter and fewer episodes before committing to doing more. It also looks better if you increase later than reduce as it then appears that you are giving more value.

Weighing up the pros and cons
Let's talk now about the pros and cons of doing a long versus a short podcast. With a short podcast you don't have to take as long in planning and recording each episode. It's something that you could do quite quickly within a day and get it out there, get it uploaded and get it published, especially if you're a solopreneur and it's just you that has to show up. You can even dedicate a day to recording several episodes in one go and scheduling them to go out weeks into the future. So, a short podcast is good for that reason and it's also good for your listeners, if your listeners have indicated that they're busy people and they would like to have the short sharp little bits of information on a regular basis. Then you are serving your customers by giving them exactly what they want.

The cons of having a shorter episode length is that it is going to be difficult for you to be able to manage interviews within that space of time. So, if you did want to interview somebody, your interview might sound very rushed if you're trying to cram everything into your regular timeframe. You may not attract that many guests willing to appear on your show for that reason too.

If you tend to go in-depth, you may find that 15 minutes doesn't give you enough time to really explore the topic and give the value that you wanted to give to your audience. Then you probably need to think about having a longer podcast rather than a shorter one.

Let's look now at doing a longer podcast. The obvious pro is that your listeners are going to feel like they're getting a lot of value from you. They can sink their teeth into the content, and you would certainly look like someone who knows their stuff and is able to deliver great value to your audience.

Being able to deliver an hour each week of really good content will certainly go towards building your authority. The risk, however, is that you may lose audience interest if you can't keep up the edutainment side of it. If you're going for one hour, you've really got to engage your listeners to keep them listening. If you're not able to do that, you're going to find that listeners will drop off and you might actually end up then losing your audience base because they may not choose to tune in for further episodes, particularly if they feel that it's too much for them or it's not interesting enough for them.

Another point to consider is, even if you can hold their interest, do they have the time to commit a full hour to you? They may be fully engaged with your content but can't carve out an hour a day to listen to it.

You will naturally find your audience based on the frequency and length of your episodes and the quality of your content. You won't be able to please everybody, but if you keep things consistent, you should be able to build up a loyal following.

The disadvantage of committing to doing a long podcast is that you've got to fill that hour if you have committed to an hour each time. Keep in mind that it is not just the time it takes to record the episode either. You need time to plan it beforehand as well.

Not only that, but you need to find enough content to last the hour each time. So just be aware of where you want to start and maybe you want to take a medium ground and start with half an hour and see how that goes. You can then decide whether you feel confident with a half-hour episode and you can manage that each time or whether you feel after some time that you'd prefer to do shorter slots. You would also then be in a position to know whether you'd be happier with shorter, sharper and snappier episodes or whether you are quite enjoying the half-hour episodes and you could easily go another half an hour each time.

Time will allow you to find your path, so don't feel you have to stick to the format you started out with. As I mentioned earlier, don't overcommit yourself in the beginning. It is better to start short and go longer than it is to start longer and have to go shorter because you just don't have the ability or the content to sustain it all the time.

However, once you pick a frequency, I would recommend that you stick with it. So, if you are committing to doing one episode a week, then make sure you do that. Make it an absolute must that you put out an episode at the frequency that you have committed to and build that into your planning schedule.

Pre-launch content
As you are getting ready to launch your podcast, I would advise that you plan and record your first five episodes so that you have some content for your first visitors to consume. You don't want to launch and send people to your podcast and there's only one episode there to listen to. Put up at least five so that you are giving them a clear picture of what your podcast is about. And by the time they've consumed that, your

next one will be ready to upload. Give them something substantial to start with as you launch.

YOUR ACTION CHALLENGE

What is your podcast format?

What is the length?

Name your first 5 podcast topics.

1.

2.

3.

4.

5.

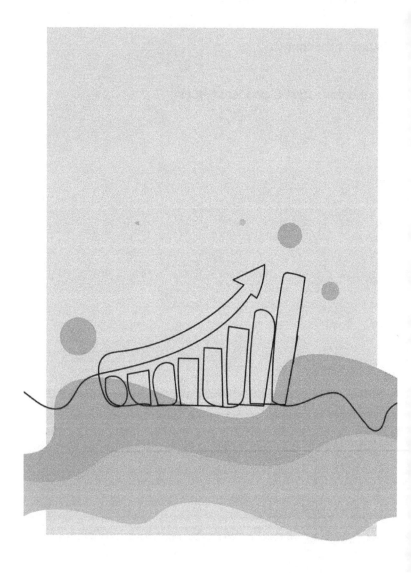

CHAPTER 7

YOUR
PROFIT STRATEGY

In this chapter, you're going to decide on your profit strategy. What is the driver for creating your podcast in terms of you making your money? Obviously, there's a reason you are putting your podcast out there. Yes, you want to deliver value for your listeners. Yes, you want to build your credibility and your authority, but ultimately you want to monetise in some way from it.

You want to be able to make it worth your while. There's got to be some kind of return on investment of your time and it's going to cost you money to produce. You have the costs of certain monthly subscriptions that you to have to pay as part of the production process. So, it makes sense that you're going to make some profit from running the podcast. Let's talk about the different ways you can go about this. There are a few different strategies that you can adopt to profit from your podcast.

Build your list
We've spoken about this before – how having a podcast can help you build your list. This isn't going to give you a direct monetary profit, but the money will come indirectly through the extra people that you get on your list that you can then market to and present your offers to. Some of your listeners can be your potential

customers. So, you can get them onto your list, and you can market to them later and you can continue marketing to them, nurturing them until you can turn them into paying customers.

Your podcast can be a list-building strategy, especially if the format you have chosen is bringing in guest speakers as well. This is going to quicken the strategy as the more guests you have on and the more speaking slots you can get on other people's podcasts, the more people you can make aware of your podcast and the faster you can grow your list.

Promote your own products/services
You may decide that your podcast is simply a vehicle for you to be able to promote your own products and services while adding value for your listeners through your excellent content.

This works very well is you chose the solo presenter format. You are the only one speaking on the podcast in each episode so you can deliver your training and teaching and promote your own products or services. There are two ways you can do this.

Brought to you by ...
You can approach this by "sponsoring" your own episode as a "Brought to you by ..." and then you mention the product that you're wanting to promote and give a little bit of information about it.

Product/service-focussed episode
Another way you can promote a particular product or service is to build the entire episode around it. So, for example, you could make an episode just about one case study on somebody that you've helped with certain

aspects of the services that you provide, and then offer that service to your listeners as a limited time offer.

A case study is an excellent way of getting people to understand on a more personal level what you do and the value you provide. People going through the same journey can relate to the pain and desire the promised outcome. The great thing is that you end up promoting your products and services all the way through the episode, but you're doing it in a way that will educate the listener, and in a way that they can relate to. It will also be enthralling and entertaining because it's told in a story format, and people love to listen to stories. So, think about ways that you can sell your products and services or make people more aware of what it is that you offer in terms of your products and services.

Sell advertising space

I've mentioned this in a previous chapter where we touched on making passive income. You can run advertisements on your podcast and get direct income from doing that by selling your airtime. You can either pitch to your local community or network to get a company to sponsor an episode. They pay to be promoted on your episode and be written into the show notes with a link to their particular product or service on their website or sales page.

Another more passive way to earn income (because you don't have to do any of the work) is to use the podcast hosting platform that you're on to place the ads for you. I use Libsyn as my podcast hosting platform. In Libsyn, you can indicate that you are open to having ads on your podcast and interested advertisers will be matched by the platform to your podcast. You get automatic advertisements on your podcast and share a 50-50 revenue share with the podcast hosting platform. That's fair because you are not actually doing anything to get the advertiser. The platform is doing it for you. Whereas if you are pitching to your own community and getting sponsors yourself, you've got to put in a lot more work and effort into creating that awareness, building the relationships with the sponsors, organising the submission of their advertisements at the right time and things like that. Of course, the upside to this method is that you get to pocket all of the revenue.

YOUR ACTION CHALLENGE

Tick the strategies you will use to monetise your podcast.

- o Build your list through guest interviews
- o Brought to you by
- o Case study
- o Self-sourced sponsors
- o Platform matched sponsors

What will you do to make this happen?

_____
_____
_____
_____
_____
_____
_____
_____
_____
_____
_____
_____
_____
_____
_____
_____
_____
_____
_____
_____

CHAPTER 8

PLANNING YOUR EPISODES

By now, you've probably realised that getting a regular podcast episode out is going to take some planning. You've also realised that you need to be consistent in both the creation and the delivery of your content in order to retain listeners.

In this chapter, we are going to look at how to plan the steps needed on a daily, weekly or monthly basis to get your content out there.

Planning your time is absolutely critical. The good news is that there are quite a lot of tools out there, especially tech tools, that can help you plan your time and get your content created in a highly efficient way.

In fact, when I first got into podcasting, I was really surprised at how easy it is to produce a podcast all by yourself with no tech knowledge and without even a professional studio. You can create your show from scratch from designing of the visuals and the brand itself through to the recording and publication of the podcast on to all the platforms that feature podcasts in some very easy steps.

So, let's look at how easy it is to create an episode. First of all, let's look at the tools you will need.

Project management software

You should start off with good project management software. You will need to be able to schedule all the tasks around getting your podcast out in as automated a way as possible. Scheduling each task that needs to happen on project management software will help you to make sure nothing gets missed and that things stay on plan.

How it works is that you can create the full workflow in the software so that nothing ever gets forgotten, then simply assign each task in the workflow to the right person to complete at the right time so that the next task can happen on time. In essence, you no longer have to rely on your memory to get things done and can operate stress-free knowing that the software is automating the entire process for you. Once the process is proven to work, you simply rinse and repeat for every episode.

There is a wide range of online time and project management tools available online and most are relatively inexpensive, especially if you have a small team. You can research the options yourself and choose whichever tools you like but I have listed a few here that I have used in the past. The one you choose will very much be down to your own personal preference.

Asana

My virtual assistant (VA) is an advocate of Asana. She loves its capability to go into depth and automate very complex processes. It a very powerful tool, very sophisticated and it can get a lot of things done as long as you know how to use it. But for me that's the problem. You need to invest quite a lot of energy into learning how to make the most out of it. And I find it visually very bland and that makes it hard for me to follow what had been assigned to who and when, etc.

So, she loves it but I'm not particularly a fan of it. That's what I mean by it being a very personal choice. You will need to go and try them out and see what works best for you.

You are going to look at some of these software programs and you're going to say, *OK, I don't get it. I don't like it. This isn't for me.* And others, you are going to look at them and say *Oh, wow. This is exactly what I need.*

Wrike

Wrike is another I have tried in the past. It's fantastic because that is so flexible in that you can build it to do whatever you want. You are basically starting with a blank slate, which might be really scary for some people, but if you really know how you want to organise things, you can set it up in exactly the way you want to run your workflow. You can get really sophisticated if you are willing to put in the initial groundwork to make it work. It's something that can really work for you.

Basecamp

Another I used in the past is Basecamp. I find it to be a very good collaboration tool and it's quite fun to use, which gets my vote every time! If you've got people across the globe and you want to communicate with them easily, Basecamp could be the way for you. You can work in Projects and in Teams. And a major thing for me is that it is highly visual. And it has got a great little section, which it calls HQ, where messages for everyone go. That's great for companywide announcements. But you can also break conversations down solely among different teams or individuals. So, you can manage different groups in different ways.

Monday

Monday is another one which is great because it's highly colourful and can be adapted to the way different people think, so you can look at tasks in different views, from linear, to card to Gantt chart views. So that's quite flexible. You can add any columns you want and pull out data in reports based on certain inputs. The Monday team is constantly adding new features and apps to it to complement the way you work.

Trello

Trello is another really good one, and one I have recently gone back to using because of its simplicity. It's so highly visual and just so easy to use. It's a card-based system, with each card being a task. You can move the card around, assign it to different people, create checklists within a card where you can tick things off as they are done. So, it can be like a mini to-do list within a to-do task. I find Trello really visual and that's the way I work. So that's the one I use.

But, as I said, just use whichever you feel the most comfortable with. There's no right or wrong project management software. You've just got to use one that works best for you and is set up in a way that you don't miss any tasks that you have coming up. The goal is for everyone to be able to work together to get your episodes planned, content created, and episodes scheduled to go live as seamlessly as possible.

Content development tools

When you are planning your content, as we covered in the previous chapters, you need to create your buckets of content and then fill those buckets with your subtopics and then fill your subtopics with your sub subtopics that become your episodes.

So you need to make sure that the topics that you cover address the questions that your customers have asked you and then, as you continue with your podcast, you're going to probably find that people are going to give you feedback and ask questions and then those questions will spur ideas for future episodes. So, it's an ever-moving, ever-growing task in a way.

You can also use social listening tools to gather more ideas based on what is trending:

eClincher: I use a platform called eClincher, which is a social media curating and scheduling tool. It allows you not only to schedule posts across all your different social media platforms but allows you to curate other people's content to share based on keyword searches. It also allows you to insert keywords to social listen to what people are talking about around those keywords. This is excellent fodder for content ideas. There are other tools that are similar like Hootsuite, Ask Edgar, etc.

Google: And even just googling works. You just search for a particular topic on Google and see what comes up in the lists.

Facebook/Instagram/LinkedIn/Twitter: And again, just put keywords or hashtags into your social media platforms and see what comes up.

There's just so many ways that you can get ideas for content. We are overloaded with information nowadays because of social media, so I don't think there's any reason you should have a lack of content. It should be more that you are overwhelmed with the amount of content that you could possibly be putting out. So, for that reason, it's important to plan by separating that content into your different buckets and then further separating it there. So at least that allows you to plan and just work with manageable chunks of content at one time.

Plan your episode structure

Now you have content planned, the next thing we want to do is look at how you're going to plan your episode structure. In other words, what order are you going to put things in within your episode.

Generally speaking, you would have some intro music that will brand your podcast playing at the beginning. This will fade into a voiceover that you can have professionally recorded narrating the podcast intro description you will have planned out by now. This will immediately speak to the listener as to whether they should be listening to your podcast or not. They need to hear that the podcast is for them and will deliver the promised transformation.

After the voiceover, you want to then come in and welcome your listeners to the podcast and say what podcast episode number it is. Then introduce your topic for the episode so your listeners know what they will be listening to and what they can expect to learn in this episode. Move on then to deliver your main content and close the episode with a summary of what was covered.

Finally, you want to thank your audience for listening and ask them to subscribe, rate and share your podcast if they liked what they were listening to. That way you can try and keep listeners coming back again.

Move on then to the outro music which will play the episode out.

Create a template to work from

Create a template (or assign a team member to do this) of this structure for every episode so you don't miss anything out. You can task someone in your team to create your show notes and script for each episode based on this template as follows:

- Fill out your show notes to describe in writing what the episode is about and bullet point the points that will be covered.
- Create some reminder content cards for you so that you have those cards ready when you're speaking. This way you aren't reading from a script but will have notes, so you don't forget to include certain information. Or it could be a ticklist.
- Set up the episode title and description in the podcast hosting platform (see later chapters).
- Key the show notes into the episode show notes section in your podcast hosting platform (see later chapters).
- Upload episode recording or batch of recordings.

Work per episode or in batches

It is a better use of everyone's time if you record a few episodes in one day (if you are a solo presenter) and process and schedule the episodes on the same day. The episodes can be scheduled for future release. They don't have to go out the day they are uploaded. We will go into how to upload and release your episodes in a later chapter. I would recommend that you block off some days each month or every three months to get that done and dedicate that time just to getting as many of your podcasts recorded for future release as you possibly can.

What are show notes?

I mentioned earlier about creating show notes. This is your episode summary or intro. It describes to interested visitors what the episode is about and entices them to listen to it.

Your show notes will include the following:

- A commanding title that entices people to listen
- Introduction describing what the episode is about and, if you have a guest, who your guest is and the topic to be discussed
- Bullet points of the main key points that listeners will learn in the episode
- Call to action to download any offer or click any link
- Reminder to subscribe, rate and share the episode
- A link to your bio or social media pages

Your show notes for the Apple platform will be slightly different as this platform has a character limit for your show notes. So, you will need to edit down your original show note for Apple.

Hopefully, this chapter has given you insights into streamlining the production of your podcasts by systemising and automating the process, outsourcing tasks to your team, if you have one, and getting your episodes recorded and uploaded efficiently using batch processing.

YOUR ACTION CHALLENGE

Research the following project management tools and content creation tools and add any more you find. List the good and bad points in the table. Make a decision as to which tool you will use.

Tool	Advantages	Disadvantages
Asana		
Wrike		
Basecamp		
Monday		
Trello		
eClincher		
Hootsuite		

Create a template design for your show notes then convert this to a templated Word document and upload it to your chosen project management software for safekeeping.

Create a template for your show episodes so that no information goes missing per episode then convert this to a templated Word document and upload it to your chosen project management software for safekeeping.

CHAPTER 9

RECORDING AND PUBLISHING YOUR PODCAST EPISODES

In this chapter, we want to master the rest of your hardware and software tech tools so that you can record, edit and publish your podcasts episodes.

My tools

I have detailed in this book only the tools I use. There are many other ways to create podcasts. You may find some better equipment, or cheaper solutions, but I am only outlining what I do for my podcasts. These are definitely good enough for you to start a podcast for sure and it may be that, as you get more serious going forward and want a more professional production, you will upgrade your equipment.

There's nothing wrong with what I am using. But if you decide you want to go more upscale later on, then you can invest in higher grade equipment like mixers that will give you more depth in your tone. However, what I outline in this book is enough to get you going and it's enough for you to sound quite professional in your podcast for at least the first year or so.

These tools allow me to record my episodes as well as my intro and outro segments for each episode, edit and slice the audio as needed, equalize the sound and stitch the intro and outro segments to the episodes automatically, host my podcast episodes with the tile visuals and show notes, and publish each episode, immediately or by scheduling, onto all key podcast platforms including my own website, Apple, Spotify and Stitcher.

So, let's break this down in terms of the hardware and the software you need.

THE HARDWARE

Microphone

You will definitely need a good microphone. For the purposes of this book, I'm not going to go into all the technical details of all the different kind of mics out there. I would suggest a USB microphone that you can just plug into your computer. You can have one that stands on your desk or has a boom arm you can clip to the side of your desk so that the microphone is hanging in front of you. The boom arm is a better way to handle it because it's not going to pick up as much noise every time you bang your desk, or you put a cup down.

It's not going to pick up those sounds as much because it won't pick up the vibration on the desk as it is not sitting on the desk in the same way a stand microphone does. I've also heard people saying that they recorded using a stand microphone on their desk and when they listened to the recording they were really confused because there was a humming sound that they just couldn't get rid of. It took them ages to work out that it was the humming and vibration of the CPU of the computer on the desk. As soon as they removed the microphone from the desk, the problem was solved.

I use a Blue Yeti microphone. It's a good mic, but it picks up every single sound. It's manageable but it's best if you can record in a very quiet environment if podcasting with this mic. Other great brands you can consider are Rode, Audio Technica and Samson.

Before you start your first recording, do a trial run to filter out any sounds you hadn't noticed might be a distraction such as any vibration, humming of an aircon and things like that.

Microphone filter
A microphone filter is something that will enrich the sound quality and take the sharpness away from your speech. This is a spongey filter placed in front of your microphone. Or you can simply put a sock over the microphone! It will just soften the sound a bit, so you are more pleasing to listen to.

Headphones
You will need headphones or earphones when you are doing interviews. Make sure you inform your interviewee to wear headphones or earphones too. These can be proper internet headphones with or without a microphone (you can plug the headphones into your Blue Yeti) or use the earphones that come with your mobile phone.

THE SOFTWARE

Recording and editing software
You're going to need recording software that enables you to edit the file to take away unwanted sections of your recording.

If you are using a Mac, then the built in GarageBand is perfect for your purposes. Audacity is a good recording and editing tool if you are using a PC. You will also need this to create your intro and outro soundbites for each episode. You can edit in the professional voiceover file using this as well. I hired a professional voice-over artist on an online platform *voices.com*. When they sent the recording back as an MP3 file, I just added it to the audio editing software to mix the intro music and the voiceover together. Then I did a separate audio recording of the same music for the outro just playing for a few seconds and then fading out to nothing. I saved both files as MP3s for later use.

If you are doing remote interviews, where the person is not sitting in the same room as you, then you will need software that will record both of you on two separate tracks. For this purpose, I use SquadCast.

SquadCast is more than just the recording tool for the interview. It's a kind of scheduling tool for the interview as well. Through the software, I can set up the agreed interview day and time and invite my interviewee into the "meeting" directly through the software. The software sends both me and the interviewee an email with login details for the "meeting". The interviewee can add this appointment to their calendar and log in at the correct timing using the calendar link provided.

In my SquadCast backend, I can see exactly who I've got lined up for interviews, the title of the podcast and when the interview will be. It's a great way for me to keep track of my interview schedule.

It also divides the interviews into past and future sessions. With the past interviews, it stores the interview recording files as individual files for each person. I can choose to mix the two files together into one MP3 file to upload to my podcast hosting platform later.

Always test the audio is working for both parties by taking a quick sample recording of both of you before you begin. The first podcast I ever did, my interviewee hadn't set the microphone settings up correctly so when I played it back, I could only hear me in the interview recording. I had to arrange to repeat the interview to correct this!

Also use the time in the beginning to go over with your interviewee any last points to make before you start recording. This helps to relax you both as well. You can have a chat with the guest and answer any questions that they have, discuss what it is you're going to be talking about so you both go into the interview fully aware and fully planned on what questions you are going to ask.

Nowadays I also use SquadCast just to record my solo episodes. If I need to edit out any mistakes, I have the option of importing the file into GarageBand to make the edits. But for the most part, I tend not to edit my podcasts and leave them naturally more authentic.

However, if you do want to edit mistakes out, here is a handy tip: When you make a mistake that you know you want to edit out later, clap your hands loudly. Later in the editing software, you will visually be able to see the rise in volume caused by the clap so you can quickly locate the place in the file and make your edit.

Sound equaliser and intro/outro editor
Podcast platforms are particular, understandably, about the sound quality of your podcasts. Your podcast audio needs to pass a certain quality test before it can be published. But not to worry. There are software tools that will help you ensure your audio quality passes the test. I use Auphonic.

Auphonic basically controls the audio quality of your podcast recording and levels out the sound so that you don't have one section louder than another. This makes for a pleasant listening experience. Auphonic will automatically adjust your recordings where it can. If your original recording is of too poor a quality, it will reject it completely and you will have to find a different recording solution. This happened to me only once, where I tried to record using Zoom. I probably had the settings wrong as many people use Zoom to record their podcasts. But for my experience, Auphonic would not accept the recording. Now that I use Squadcast and GarageBand, I don't have the problem.

Once you set up an Auphonic account, you get a certain number of hours of recording a month free. If you exceed the allotted number of hours, you will have to upgrade to a paid plan. Once you have set up your plan, you upload your episode recording to Auphonic and let it work its magic.

What is great about Auphonic is that you can also upload your intro and outro snippets one time and instruct Auphonic to edit them onto the front and back of every episode you upload. It's then done for you automatically. It's a great little time saver.

Podcast hosting platform
Your podcasting platform is the software that hosts your completed podcast episodes and the artwork to your show. It also distributes your episode content in the correct format to all instructed podcast platforms such as Apple and Spotify.

For this, I use a platform call Libsyn. It basically does everything that you need for get your podcast distributed. It links with your Auphonic account so that every time you run your episode through Auphonic, it will automatically place the completed file, with intro and outro included, into your Libsyn account. You simply pick up the file there and complete the episode creation process by adding your artwork (you can choose the same tile each time or design a new one per episode) and show notes (there is a separate field to key in the shorter version for Apple) and scheduling the date of release.

Do note that when you choose immediate release, you will not be able to find your show on every platform immediately. It will take some time for it to be approved, especially the first launch. Depending on the platform, this can be a few minutes, a few hours or a few days.

You can also publish each episode on your own website simply by copying the code that Libsyn will supply for the episode and pasting it into the page on your site.

As mentioned in earlier chapters, you can agree to have advertisers on your podcast. This is not compulsory though. If you do, and ads are placed on your podcast, you share the revenue with Libsyn.

Once you get all these accounts set up and synced, it takes a few minutes to upload and release each new episode.

YOUR ACTION CHALLENGE

Sign up for the following platforms and record your login details below:

- Podcast hosting: **Libsyn**
- Audio editing**: Auphonic**
- Podcast episode recording (especially for guest interviews): **SquadCast**
- Audio recording and editing:
  GarageBand (Mac)
  Audacity (PC)

Libsyn will automatically list your podcast show on certain platforms including Spotify. You must list manually on the following platforms. Do so now and record your login details.
- Apple podcasts
- Stitcher

Hire a voiceover to record your show introduction. You can try *voices.com*

When you get the recording back, create your intro music with the voiceover introduction and your outro music soundbites (or outsource this task to a professional). Save the files in MP3 format in the Apps folder in your computer so that Auphonic can find them. Add these files to your Auphonic platform so that they will be stitched to the front and back of every episode automatically.

Choose your hardware. Decide what microphone, microphone filter and headphones/earphones you will use and purchase them if needed.

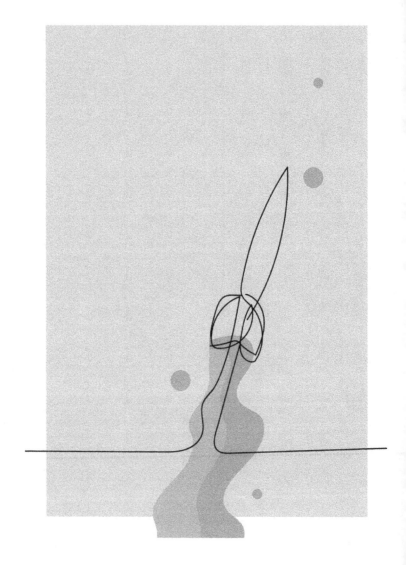

CHAPTER 10

IT'S LAUNCH DAY

Now that you've mastered the tech tools and recorded your first five episodes, it's time to start planning your launch day.

Start to plan your media attention. Think about the touchpoints you can use to connect with your audience.

Get media attention
To get media attention, there are a few ways that are open to you.

Firstly, tap on the free social media reach you already have. Start putting out teaser posts for a few weeks leading up to launch day to get people interested in and aware of what you are planning.

Here are some posts you can try:

Before launch
- Hint at what's coming up
- Behind the scenes preparation of your episodes
- Talk about the tech you are using such as showing off your microphone
- Show off your show artwork

- o Send people to your landing page to register interest in knowing when the launch happens (build your list)
- o Join Facebook Groups and create relationships. Share related content
- o When people engage take the conversation out of the group and tell them about your podcast
- o Send updates to your existing email lists and send them to your landing page to sign up to be notified of the release date.
- o Make a big announcement of the launch date

After launch

- o Record a video showing people how they can subscribe to your show once it's live.
- o Each time you have a guest speaker, announce the upcoming session to everyone.
- o Once its live, send the link out to everyone.

Launch day

On launch day, make sure the show is live (remember it can take a few days to appear) and then drive everyone to Apple to listen, share, and subscribe. Create a buzz about people listening to your show and how you are advancing in the rankings. Encourage more people to visit to drive rankings higher.

Screenshot and share on social media your rankings as they increase and communicate how excited you are that your podcast is being listened to by people. Share at every opportunity on all your platforms to drive people over through the next few days. Communicate your link through all your social media platforms, on your email signatures, and thank you pages.

YOUR ACTION CHALLENGE

Plan your pre-launch media posts. Tick each below as you do them.

Before launch
- o Hint at what's coming up
- o Behind the scenes preparation of your episodes
- o Talk about the tech you are using such as showing off your microphone
- o Show off your show artwork
- o Send people to your landing page to register interest in knowing when the launch happens (build your list)
- o Join Facebook Groups and create relationships. Share related content
- o When people engage take the conversation out of the group and tell them about your podcast
- o Send updates to your existing email lists and send them to your landing page to sign up to be notified of the release date
- o Make a big announcement of the launch date

After launch
- o Record a video showing people how they can subscribe to your show once it's live.
- o Each time you have a guest speaker, announce the upcoming session to everyone.
- o Once its live, send the link out to everyone.

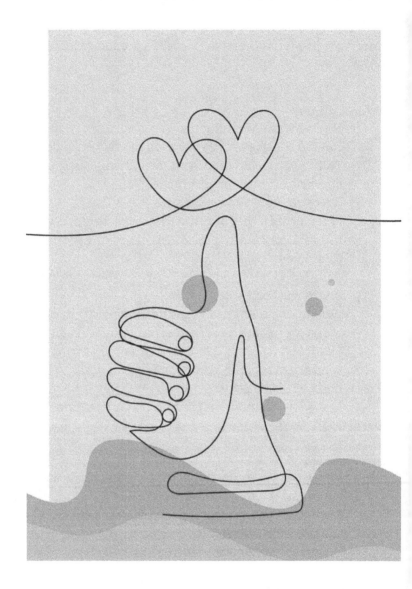

CHAPTER 11

KEEP PEOPLE COMING

Congratulations! You now have your podcast up and running and launched for the world to see. What do you do now?

Firstly, use your project management platform to ensure that you continue to plan, record and release your podcast episodes on a regular basis so that you can build your audience and your library of episodes and get people coming back time and again to consume your content.

List on more podcast listening platforms

How do you keep that attention? How do you keep people coming back? How do your grow your brand? Over time, you want to be looking at submitting your podcast to even more directories. Libsyn allows you to automatically post to a certain number of podcast platforms but this number is limited. Consider the many more podcast directories you could apply to. Do a search online for these and submit your podcast a few a week. Or to fast-track the process, outsource this task to your VA. This will give your podcast a greater reach to people that are using these other platforms. The more directories you list your podcast on, the easier it will be for people to come across your podcast.

Use #hashtags

Create a hashtag for your podcast and place this on everything you post. There is a great way to do this by creating a shortcut for all your hashtags through your mobile phone keyboard. As you post on your social media platforms from your phone, hit the shortcut key and all your hashtags will appear. No more keying in a long list of hashtags every time!

Ask your listeners to screenshot and share

Another thing you can do to create more awareness is to ask your listeners to screenshot that they're listening to your podcast and ask them to share with their audience as well.

Brand everything with your podcast link

I've covered this before, but it is an important point to repeat: Put your podcast link on everything you can from your website, thank you pages and email signature to your posts. If you can place a link anywhere, do so.

Consider guest interviews

As mentioned before, this is a great way to double your reach with every podcast.

Get active on social media

It's a complete promotion game. Promote, promote, promote at every opportunity and slowly build your listener base over time. Show up regularly on social media and feature stories about your podcast in different ways. Feature your guests, show behind the scenes views, etc.

Keep the awareness and interest going until people eventually say *OK, I need to go and listen to this podcast. I've heard about it so much.*

Ask for the subscribe

Ask that people don't just visit but subscribe. At the end of every podcast episode you do, remember to ask your listeners to subscribe so they know when the next episode is released and will come back to listen again.

Keeping track of progress

As you build your base, you can keep track of the success of your show on your Libsyn platform. In your account, you will find a section that details your stats - how many listeners you have, how many downloads there have been in a particular month or a selected period of time.

If your numbers start to go down, then you know that it is time to do some extra promotion to bring in listeners again. That's the way that you keep the love coming and grow your listener base for your podcast.

Keep podcasting!

.

YOUR ACTION CHALLENGE

Create your hashtags shortcut on your mobile phone keyboard.

Put your podcast link on the following:

- o Email signature
- o Promotional social media posts
- o Thank-you pages

Find the section on Libsyn where you can track your numbers. Record your figures here each month.

Year	Jan	Feb	Mar	Apr	May	Jun	Jul	Aug	Sep	Oct	Nov	Dec
No. of Downloads												
Year	Jan	Feb	Mar	Apr	May	Jun	Jul	Aug	Sep	Oct	Nov	Dec
No. of Downloads												

Scan me